God's Word or Your Wand:
Recognize and Remove Witchcraft from Your Life

Dedication

This book is dedicated to all people everywhere – all of whom God loves deeply. (That includes **you!**)

Table of Contents

Forewords

Deamon Scapin, Pastor
Triumph Church D.C.

My Dear Friend,

There comes a moment in every genuine journey of faith when we must pause and ask ourselves: *Am I truly walking in the light, or have I unknowingly allowed shadows to creep into my path?*

In this powerful and profoundly necessary book, Sabrina Hamm has offered a faithful service to the Body of Christ. She has dared to shine a bright light on territories the enemy has long sought to keep dark – areas where spiritual compromise has been cleverly rebranded, allowing witchcraft, rebellion, and idolatry to settle quietly into modern life under the guise of "self-care", "spirituality," or "personal growth".

We live in an era where the ancient practices of divination, sorcery, and seeking power apart from the Creator have been sanitized and reintroduced as acceptable (even fashionable) ways to achieve fulfillment. The core message of this volume is a bold confrontation of this deception: You cannot mix light and darkness and expect to honor God or walk in His best for your life.

This is not a book of condemnation. It is a spiritual searchlight motivated by deep, corrective love. Through careful teaching, each chapter breaks down these deceptive practices – revealing their roots, how they are masked today and, critically, why they stand in opposition to God's holy Word.

This book calls you to the path of freedom found only in obedience. When we choose to obey God, we step directly into the abundant blessing He promises. As the Scriptures remind us, obedience ensures we are blessed in the city and the country, in our work, and in our families. It guarantees that we will be the head and not the tail, lending to nations but borrowing from none.

This journey requires courage, as our struggle is not against flesh and blood, but against spiritual forces of evil in the heavenly realms. Therefore, I urge you, as you turn these pages, to take hold of the Call to Action, the Prayer, and the Promise Scripture offered in each chapter. Use them as tools to put on the full armor of God and to stand firm. If a chapter makes you say, "Ouch!", take heart! That conviction is the Holy Spirit warning and rescuing you from danger. God is simply asking you to honor Him by living in a way that brings life to you and to others.

May the truths contained within these pages give you the courage to take a real inventory of your life and cut away anything unpleasing to God. May you move forward in freedom, firmly rooted in the authority of Christ, knowing that you have already overcome the evil one because the Word of God lives in you.

May the Lord bless you as you transition from blind spots to blessed clarity. The ultimate choice presented to you, the reader, is stark but clear: God's Word or Your Wand.

Adiyb Muhammad
Bestselling Author and Transformational Coach

There are moments in life when a book does more than inform: It reaches into places we didn't realize needed healing, correction, or clarity. This is one of those books.

When I first encountered Sabrina Hamm's manuscript, I felt something beyond interest. I felt recognition. I saw the ways so many people I've spoken to – friends, family, believers, seekers – have unknowingly opened doors in their lives simply because they were searching for peace, identity, or comfort. I felt the weight of how easy it is in today's world to drift into practices that feel innocent, but pull us away from the God who loves us.

And I also felt relief. Relief that someone had the courage, the compassion, and the spiritual sensitivity to address these issues with honesty and grace.

Sabrina's writing is not accusatory. It's not judgmental. It feels like the voice of someone who cares – someone who wants to see you free, whole, clear-minded, and spiritually protected. The way she breaks down each practice, the history, the Scripture, the call to action, and the prayers is the work of someone who genuinely wants to lead people back to the heart of God.

For me, this book brought reminders of my own journey – moments when God gently corrected me, opened my eyes, or called me deeper. And that's what I believe will happen for every reader. Not condemnation. Not fear. But awakening. Alignment. A deeper sense of spiritual responsibility and intimacy with God.

If you allow it, this book will touch you. It will challenge you. It will grow you. And most importantly, it will draw you closer to the One who has been pursuing your heart from the very beginning.

I am honored to stand alongside Sabrina's message and to witness the impact this work will surely have on all who read it.

Acknowledgements

To My Husband: Thank you for encouraging and supporting me from the moment I said I wanted to write this book. Your support never wavered throughout the entire process – something that has been true throughout our entire marriage. Your help and love are invaluable. As the theme song of The Golden Girls says, "Thank you for being a frieeeeend!" ☺ I love you, and I'm grateful to have you in my corner in all walks of life.

To My Children: Thank you for being so positive when I told you I wanted to write a book. You always smiled or said something encouraging whenever I talked about it, and you regularly checked on me to ask about the progress. Even though this book was written with a wide audience in mind, I hope in writing it that I've personally made you proud. As I always say, "Your mother loves you! That's me!" ♥

To all the family members and people who were an encouragement throughout the drafting process (most notably my mother and brothers): Thank you tremendously. Every bit of encouragement and kindness helped me to make it to the finish line, and now you're reading the finished result! When I think of blessings, I think of you.

To Mr. Adiyb: Thank you for your joyous instruction, wisdom, kindness, and patience while spurring my husband and me on to achieve big things. You have been consistent and generous with your knowledge and time, and you are one of the world's best cheerleaders! I owe you a pair of pom poms.

To Pastors Deamon and Kristine Scapin, and Apostle Deborah Jones: Thank you for being integrous, friendly, and approachable leaders. I assure you it is a compliment when I say, "Thank you for being normal" in a world when so many church leaders are unscrupulous, pretentious, and unbiblical. You ought to be marked for your excellent leadership.

And finally, but most importantly, to the Lord Jesus Christ: My hope is that the writing of this book will bring people closer to you. Thank you for using me right along with all the other flawed people throughout history, and thank you for being kind and faithful in my life. As a lyric in the song by the great CeCe Winans says, "Any good that I've done, and all that I do, it's all because of you."

Introduction

David and Tiffany met at the party of a mutual friend. It was obvious from their first encounter that there was a spark. After spending lots of time chatting with random people and hanging around the appetizer tables, David drummed up the courage to start a conversation with Tiffany. They talked with ease and, before they knew it, they'd exchanged social media information and began communicating online. Direct messages flew back and forth for weeks, which eventually turned into text messages and video calls. David and Tiffany soon exchanged telephone numbers and went on their first date. That's when they knew there was something special happening. After a few more dates, they began seeing one another exclusively. The initial spark between David and Tiffany continued to grow over time as they got to learn more about one another and spend more time together. After about six months of dating, they began meeting one another's families. It was evident that love was in the air, and the two became inseparable. David proposed to Tiffany on Christmas Eve about one year after they began seeing one another exclusively. After months of planning, they married in the fall of the following year. David and Tiffany were now husband and wife! What a happy feeling!

David was the best husband to Tiffany. He was thoughtful, caring, and looked after Tiffany's needs in every manner possible. All of Tiffany's friends told her how lucky she was to have David, and how they wanted their significant others to be just like him. Tiffany knew she had a great guy, and counted herself lucky. The problem was, after the first two years of marriage, Tiffany began to sense a growing hint of — SOMETHING. Was it dissatisfaction? Sure, David was a great partner, provider, and friend, but he was so PRACTICAL and, well, a bit BORING! Where was the excitement? Where were the butterflies and the spark she felt before? They seemed to be gone, and were replaced with something that felt more like simple familiarity.

One Tuesday, as was her custom, Tiffany headed to her local gym to get in a good workout when she saw "The Guy". The Guy was another gym goer Tiffany saw regularly. He was always smiling and friendly toward Tiffany, but was never inappropriate. After a few brief "Hello, how are you?" greetings to The Guy over some time, Tiffany was surprised when he stopped her one day to have a conversation. As The Guy asked where she was from and what she did for a living, Tiffany noticed a bit more about him than before. How white his teeth were. How his eyes sparkled when he spoke. Tiffany quickly wiped away those thoughts and kept her mind on the conversation at hand before it ended a few moments later.

Visit after visit to the gym, Tiffany and The Guy held short conversations that began to grow a bit longer each time. Before they knew it, they left the gym one day to grab a coffee from the local shop. Although Tiffany was having to push away random thoughts about The Guy when she was doing other things, she figured, "It's just coffee. I'm not doing anything wrong. After all, he sees I'm wearing a wedding ring." But one coffee turned into another, and then another, and then another. Tiffany and The Guy exchanged phone numbers, but Tiffany didn't tell her husband, David. She just kept telling herself, "We're not doing anything wrong. The Guy told Tiffany, "Don't be so paranoid. We're just two friends hanging out!" Time passed and, before she knew it, Tiffany was going out with The Guy more and more, and not just to coffee. Her conscious gnawed at her every time, but she always found a way to excuse her behavior. Then, one day, the inevitable happened: The Guy and Tiffany crossed the line physically. The guilt consumed Tiffany for weeks – so much so that she eventually had to break the news to David. David was absolutely crushed at the news of his wife's infidelity. The toll of Tiffany's infidelity weighed heavily on their marriage, and there were periods of time when conversations were hard and feelings were raw. However, David vowed to remain in the marriage and reconcile with Tiffany. Through counseling, numerous difficult talks, and a lot of love, David and Tiffany were able to stand the test of time and live as a loving and committed couple. Tiffany came to realize what she had all along – a loving, committed, and faithful husband.

While this was a story about a marital relationship gone wrong, it is an example of a deeper spiritual issue that is the crux of this book. Let's look at two Scriptures to get started and gain some understanding:

"For your Maker is your husband –
the Lord Almighty is his name – the Holy One of
Israel is your Redeemer; he is called the God of all
the earth." (Isaiah 54:5, NIV)

"Husbands, love your wives, just as Christ loved the
church and gave himself up for her to make her
holy, cleansing her by the washing with water
through the word, and to present her to himself as a
radiant church, without stain or wrinkle or any
other blemish, but holy and blameless. In this same
way, husbands ought to love their wives as their own
bodies. He who loves his wife loves himself. After all,
no one ever hated their own body, but they feed and
care for their body, just as Christ does the church
– for we are members of his body. 'For this reason a
man will leave his father and mother and be united
to his wife, and the two will become one flesh.' This
is a profound mystery – but I am talking about
Christ and the church." (Ephesians 5:25-32, NIV)

We can see from these two Scriptures that, as Christian believers, we are not just "spiritual people". We are considered the living, breathing bride of Christ. We (the bride) are in covenant with Christ (the husbandman/groom), just like a bride and groom enter into covenant when they marry one another. There are examples throughout the Bible of the church (Christian believers) being called "the bride" and God the Father being called "the husbandman". God takes covenants very seriously, and therefore used examples of covenant throughout His Word.

"That's really interesting, Sabrina, but what does that have to do with this book?"

I'm glad you asked! Think about this: If Christ is our bridegroom and the lover of our souls, then our allegiance is to Him above all else. Making binding vows to someone or something that is in opposition to Christ is like having a side relationship while you're married! To state it clearly, acts of rebellion and witchcraft are likened to committing spiritual adultery.

James 4:4 puts it bluntly:

> *"You adulterous people, don't you know that friendship with the world means enmity against God? Therefore, anyone who chooses to be a friend of the world becomes an enemy of God." (James 4:4, NIV)*

In today's language, that is a call to stop cheating on God and taking part in the things of this world.

Being a Christian is about entering into the most intimate relationship possible with God as your Heavenly Father, Jesus Christ as your Lord and Savior, and the Holy Spirit as your comfort and guide (three in one)! Even if you are a male, you can still be a bride – the bride of Christ! Spiritually speaking, God does not want to see His bride dabbling with another love. God does not just love the world in general; He loves you INDIVIDUALLY. He gave

His life not just for humanity en masse, but for you
PERSONALLY.

"But God demonstrates his own love for us in this:
While we were still sinners, Christ died for us."
(Romans 5:8, NIV)

"I have been crucified with Christ and I no longer
live, but Christ lives in me. The life I now live in the
body, I live by faith in the Son of God, who loved
me and gave himself for me." (Galatians 2:20, NIV)

The purpose of this book is to help you identify any acts of
witchcraft in your life that are hidden in plain sight. In
other words, you may be participating in things you never
knew had origins in paganism and witchcraft, and are
offensive to God.

Merriam-Webster, the world-famous dictionary, defines
"witchcraft" as:
1. "The use of sorcery or magic.
2. Communication with the devil or with a familiar.
3. Rituals and practices that incorporate belief in magic
   and that are associated especially with neo-pagan
   traditions and religions.
4. A tradition or religion that involves the practice of
   witchcraft.

Britannica defines "witchcraft" as, "The exercise or
invocation of alleged supernatural powers to control
people or events."

Many well-meaning people who earnestly love God – or
who at least want to do what is right and don't want to
offend God – have no idea that some of their actions and
involvements are directly offending God. That is because
the enemy has rebranded much of today's rebellion
(witchcraft) as "self-care," "spirituality," and
"empowerment." I am not attempting to say that

everything is wrong, or that you're not supposed to have any fun in life. However, I want to make you aware of some things to which you may have been oblivious. We all have blind spots in our lives. That's why we need one another to help us see clearly what we may have been missing.

How This Book Works
Each chapter will shine a light on a specific practice and break down:
1. **Where it came from** (its history and spiritual roots).
2. **How it's typically used today** (and how the enemy has rebranded it).
3. **Why it goes against God's Word** (with Scripture to back it up).
4. **A Call to Action** (to apply what you've learned).
5. **A Prayer** (asking God to help you move forward).
6. **One or More Promise Scriptures** (giving you truth to stand on as you take decisive actions).

As you read, keep in mind that this book is meant as correction and not condemnation. While some of this information may initially be difficult to swallow or step on your toes, my prayer is that you will not only recognize what needs to be cut from your life, but that you also have the courage to take appropriate action because of your desire to honor God.

"Hearing that Jesus had silenced the Sadducees, the Pharisees got together. One of them, an expert in the law, tested him with this question: 'Teacher, which is the greatest commandment in the Law?' Jesus replied: 'Love the Lord your God with all your heart and with all your soul and with all your mind. This is the first and greatest commandment. And the second is like it: Love your neighbor as yourself. All the Law and the Prophets hang on these two commandments.'" (Matthew 22:34-40, NIV)

Let's start this journey of freedom right here and now. LET'S GO!

Call to Action: Decide you will set aside at least 10 minutes each day to read this book until you've read it in its entirety. Ten minutes is an attainable amount of time that shouldn't derail your day. Grant yourself those 10 minutes to help shift your perspective in a different direction.

Prayer: "Lord, there may be something in this book that will help me get closer to you. Help me to be open to receive the truth that comes from your Word and your Spirit. Help me to consider the words in this book and take a real inventory of my life. If anything needs to change, give me the courage to take appropriate action. I want to honor you above all else. In Jesus' name I pray, amen." (Amen means, "So be it.")

Promise Scripture: *"But whoever looks intently into the perfect law that gives freedom, and continues in it – not forgetting what they have heard, but doing it – they will be blessed in what they do." (James 1:25, NIV)*

Chapter 1: Witchcraft in All Its Forms

"For rebellion is as the sin of witchcraft, and stubbornness is as iniquity and idolatry . . ." (1 Samuel 15:23a, NKJV)

What is the Bible's take on witchcraft? Simply put, witchcraft is synonymous with stubbornness and rebellion. The core of witchcraft is a desire for control – to get what we want, when we want, how we want, and by means outside of God's will. Witchcraft says, "I'll pull a card, wave some smoke, or recite this spell because I need to make something happen" instead of living by, "Lord, let Your will be done."

Witchcraft is not always an obvious thing like casting a spell or using potions (although it can be those things). Witchcraft can also involve subtle practices, and can be hidden in your daily activities. It is possible there is witchcraft in your life or in the lives of those you love, but it is disguised as something normal and innocent.

As mentioned, we'll be looking at specific areas of witchcraft in each chapter of this book. But for now, let's see how it all got started.

Witchcraft goes all the way back to the earliest civilizations on earth. One of the first known locations of occult activity was ancient Mesopotamia (Babylon). The Babylonians practiced divination, astrology, and spellcasting as part of their religious rituals. They believed their gods communicated through signs in the stars, omens, and dreams – often interpreted by sorcerers and priests.

Babylon is referenced in Scripture as a symbol of rebellion and confusion. (See Genesis Chapter 11 and Revelation Chapters 17 and 18 if you want to get the specific details.)

In Egypt, their magicians and sorcerers mimicked God's power as noted in the book of Exodus. You may remember Pharaoh's magicians who turned staffs into snakes.

"So Moses and Aaron went to Pharaoh and did just as the Lord commanded. Aaron threw his staff down in front of Pharaoh and his officials, and it became a snake. Pharaoh then summoned wise men and sorcerers, and the Egyptian magicians also did the same things by their secret arts: Each one threw down his staff and it became a snake. But Aaron's staff swallowed up their staffs." (Exodus 7:10-12, NIV)

God warned Israel not to adopt the practices of the Canaanites, which included child sacrifice, spellcasting, necromancy (the practice of communicating with the dead), and divination (the practice of seeking knowledge of the future by some unknown spiritual means).

"When thou art come into the land which the Lord thy God giveth thee, thou shalt not learn to do after the abominations of those nations. There shall not be found among you any one that maketh his son or his daughter to pass through the fire, or that useth divination, or an observer of times, or an enchanter, or a witch. Or a charmer, or a consulter with familiar spirits, or a wizard, or a necromancer. For all that do these things are an abomination unto the Lord: and because of these abominations the Lord thy God doth drive them out from before thee. Thou shalt be perfect with the Lord thy God. For these nations, which thou shalt possess, hearkened unto observers of times, and unto diviners: but as for thee, the Lord thy God hath not suffered thee so to do." (Deuteronomy 18:9-14, KJV)

These were spiritual systems designed to replace trust in God with rituals of power and control.

Over time, witchcraft evolved, but it never went away. Paganism flourished in the Greek and Roman empires. People worshiped gods and goddesses and called upon them for love, war, health, fertility, and overall good fortune through charms, potions, and rituals. Sorcery and divination were common. Even emperors had their own personal astrologers.

Medieval Europe gave us an image of witches that persists today – potions, cauldrons, and flying on brooms. "Witch" (from Old English "wicce" or "wicca") originally meant "wise one" or "one who practices sorcery." Today, some people still practice Wicca (a religion based on nature, paganism, and a belief in multiple deities).

No doubt, there is a great deal of evidence throughout history that witchcraft was an ongoing practice. Today, some groups try to rebrand the title of witchcraft, but it is still the same ungodly rebellion cloaked in the sentiment, "Just do you!"

Witchcraft has slid into modern culture under the guise of "spirituality" or "another way to God." Others reference the "divine feminine", "manifesting," and other practices. Social media promotes things like tarot readings, horoscopes, manifestation circles, and more. These things are not harmless spiritual practices, nor do they represent "another way to God" as some may believe. I have to tell you plainly: They are evangelistic tools for the devil, and are a direct slap in the face of God. We must reject witchcraft, no matter how normal it looks or acceptable it is to others. I hope you choose to do as it says in Ephesians 5:11 (NIV):

> *"Have nothing to do with the fruitless deeds of darkness, but rather expose them."*

That's right! It's time for us to do some exposing! In other words, we're going to look at some specific practices people involve themselves in today, and we're going to determine whether they're harmless or evil. There is no in between.

Call to Action: Pray the following prayer.

Prayer: "Jesus, as I dive into reading this book, I am asking that you prepare me to receive the truths that will be presented. Open my heart only to you, your Word, and your truth through the power of the Holy Spirit. Cover me, Lord Jesus. I put my trust in you. Help me understand that you are greater than any force that may be in the world, so I do not need to fear. Prepare me to understand the truth, take action to turn away from any witchcraft in my life, and experience a real relationship with you. Help me to stand strong and firm when people in my life may not initially understand when my actions begin to change. Jesus, I pray this prayer in your name, amen."

Promise Scripture: *"The God of peace will soon crush Satan under your feet. The grace of our Lord Jesus be with you." (Romans 16:20, NIV)*

Chapter 2: Fraternities and Sororities

"But I tell you, do not swear an oath at all: either by heaven, for it is God's throne; or by the earth, for it is his footstool; or by Jerusalem, for it is the city of the Great King. And do not swear by your head, for you cannot make even one hair white or black. All you need to say is simply 'Yes' or 'No'; anything beyond this comes from the evil one." (Matthew 5:34-37, NIV)

Fraternities and sororities are extremely popular today, and have been for centuries. It is possible you are in one, or you know at least one person who is. Greek letter organizations present themselves as valuable networks and sources of tradition and community, but underneath those seemingly positive attributes are oaths, rituals, and allegiances that are spiritually compromising for anyone who wants to honor God and have a relationship with Jesus Christ. Many of the traditions of fraternities and sororities are rooted in Freemasonry and pagan practices, and their culture often promotes idolatry, immorality, and secrecy – all of which run counter to the Word of God.

The first ever fraternity was established as Phi Beta Kappa in 1776 at the College of William & Mary. It began as a secret society with rituals, mottos, and initiation ceremonies, but later rebranded itself as an honor society focused on academics. During the 19th Century, dozens of fraternities formed on college campuses, adopting Greek letters, ritual initiation, and secret handshakes. Black Greek Letter Organizations (BGLOs) began establishing themselves in the early 1900s due to racial segregation disallowing their participation in other groups – examples of which include the Alpha Phi Alpha fraternity established in 1906 and the Alpha Kappa Alpha sorority established in 1908. The nine collective historically Black Greek-letter organizations (BGLOs) are often called the "Divine 9". (See how the devil likes to take something attributable to God's nature and apply it to something concerning himself? God is divine, but there is nothing divine about the devil.)

The first ever sorority of any type was Alpha Delta Pi, established in 1851 at Wesleyan Female College. It was initially a secret society, and later became the model for future women's Greek organizations.

Many people will likely say, "But Sabrina, I only joined my Greek organization for the brotherhood (or sisterhood)! We do a lot of good in the community, and I always meet my fellow Greeks wherever I go. I even got a job because of my involvement with my Greek organization!" I liken this to those involved in organized crime. Some of the most hardened gangsters and criminals will organize turkey giveaways for Thanksgiving, toy drives for Christmas, and do things for the community throughout the year. But does that change the fact that they are still gangsters and criminals? Absolutely not. While you are not a criminal if you're involved in a fraternity or sorority, you are still taking part in something that has roots and tenets that are in opposition to the Creator of the universe. And if you consider yourself a Christian, you're not Greek (unless you were actually born in Greece or to Greek parents). Rather, you're a citizen of heaven! You're a peculiar person! Chosen! Royal! Holy! (See 1 Peter 2:9.) Your allegiance to Christ should govern everything you do in this life. Nothing should compromise that.

People involved in fraternities and sororities are required to take oaths of loyalty to the organization with which they are pledging. Some of the oaths are even sealed with rituals. These oaths bind members to the organization in ways that can rival their loyalty to Christ, and most participants never bat an eyelash or raise an eyebrow.

"It's not that deep, Sabrina," you may say. Well, let's keep looking deeper.

Greek organizations often claim to be a person's highest loyalty – sometimes saying things like "brotherhood for life" or "sisterhood for life." This can create ill-advised allegiances, with some people trusting in their connections with their organization and its activities above their relationships with God. It may not be a conscious, intentional decision, but it often happens. Participation in Greek life can also foster pride in some people who find their sense of identity (or a large part of it) by being involved in such an organization.

> *"You shall have no other gods before me." (Exodus 20:3, NIV)*

While you may never deliberately say, "I value my Greek organization above God," your actions may state otherwise. Some people spend more time taking part in Greek activities than they do in worship of God, reading His Word, and other God-centered activities. Others trust in their organization to "hook them up with the right opportunity" more than asking God to lead and guide them. Some people won't marry a potential life partner if they are not involved in Greek life in some capacity because, "They just won't understand." These examples should be causes for several pauses.

Greek letter organizations have ritual roots in paganism and Freemasonry. Many borrowed their initiation rituals, secrecy, and structure directly from Freemasonry, which we will get into in the next chapter. This includes the use of esoteric (exclusive) symbols, candles, chants, and even mock "death and rebirth" ceremonies. These practices parallel occult traditions rather than biblical worship. As someone who wants to be pleasing to God and have a relationship with him, what business do you have being involved with something that has its origins in the occult?

"Do not be yoked together with unbelievers. For what do righteousness and wickedness have in common? Or what fellowship can light have with darkness? What harmony is there between Christ and Belial? Or what does a believer have in common with an unbeliever? What agreement is there between the temple of God and idols? For we are the temple of the living God. As God has said: 'I will live with them and walk among them, and I will be their God, and they will be my people.' Therefore, 'Come out from them and be separate,' says the Lord. 'Touch no unclean thing, and I will receive you.' And, 'I will be a Father to you, and you will be my sons and daughters,' says the Lord Almighty." (2 Corinthians 6:14-18, NIV)

Hazing

The University of Colorado Boulder defines hazing as "any activity that is condition upon recruitment, admission, affiliation, or continued participation in a group that humiliates, degrades, abuses, or endangers someone, regardless of consent or a person's willingness to participate." (Source: https://www.colorado.edu/ova/examples-hazing)

While most Greek organizations have a Code of Ethics and Conduct that prohibits the practice of hazing, that usually does not stop the practice from happening. I recently heard about a case of hazing that resulted in the death of a young man in Louisiana. He was punched in the chest several times with boxing gloves, which led to him having what appeared to be a seizure and collapsing. The young man was later taken to the hospital (after the leaders of the hazing ritual allegedly failed to initially call for medical help) and was pronounced dead. His parents, family, and friends are now grieving his senseless loss.

While I know all hazing does not result in death, it always offers humiliation, degradation, and physical harm whenever it does occur. These practices contradict Christ's command to love and build up one another.

Additionally, Greek life is often associated with drunkenness, sexual immorality, and partying. While not every group is the same, the culture of Greek life often normalizes sin.

> "Do not let any unwholesome talk come out of your mouths, but only what is helpful for building others up according to their needs, that it may benefit those who listen." (Ephesians 4:29, NIV)

> "Nor should there be obscenity, foolish talk or coarse joking, which are out of place, but rather thanksgiving." (Ephesians 5:4, NIV)

> "The acts of the flesh are obvious: sexual immorality, impurity and debauchery; idolatry and witchcraft; hatred, discord, jealousy, fits of rage, selfish ambition, dissensions, factions and envy; drunkenness, orgies, and the like. I warn you, as I did before, that those who live like this will not inherit the kingdom of God." (Galatians 5:19-21, NIV)

Greek life also thrives on secrecy and exclusivity (who's "in" and who's "out"). This contradicts the inclusive call of the Gospel where every Christ follower is part of the family of God. Members of Greek organizations often adopt a new identity centered on their fraternity/sorority letters, chants, line number, and traditions. This can overshadow their identity in Christ.

> "Therefore if any man be in Christ, he is a new creature: old things are passed away; behold, all things are become new." (2 Corinthians 5:17, KJV)

God takes vows seriously. Covenant is His idea. Binding oneself to a group that demands lifelong allegiance is in opposition to your relationship with Christ. Any group that demands such a requirement should make you stop, pause, and reflect on the reason for such a necessity. The only one to whom you should make a lifelong commitment (other than God Himself) is your God-given spouse. Otherwise, your course of action should be as we read in Ephesians 5:11: Expose the darkness! Do not conform to it.

Call to Action:
Physical/Practical Steps
These show, in the natural, that you no longer align with the organization:
- Formally resign in writing: Many fraternities and sororities have a resignation process. Writing a letter/email to the national office or local chapter helps to make the break official.
- Return or destroy paraphernalia: Give back or get rid of items like paddles, Greek letters, pins, books, and clothing tied to the organization. This isn't just symbolic; you are cutting physical ties. (Consider Acts 19:18-19 where new believers burned sorcery scrolls.) Do not give the items to someone else. TRASH them! DESTROY them!
- Cut off active involvement: Stop attending meetings, events, or participating in rituals/ceremonies.
- Step away from alumni ties: If there's a network or social club with which you are connected, decline membership or participation. You don't have to disown people – just your involvement in the organization with which you both have been a part.

Spiritual Steps
These are just as important, because fraternities and sororities often involve oaths, vows, and rituals that have spiritual weight.
- Repentance: Confess to God that joining was wrong.

- Renounce oaths and vows: Pray specifically to break any oath, vow, or covenant you spoke or agreed to. Ask God to fill the places in your life where the fraternity or sorority used to be. For example: "In Jesus' name, I renounce and break every oath, vow, and covenant I made to [Fraternity/Sorority Name]. I declare that my allegiance is to Jesus Christ alone."
- Ask God to cancel spiritual ties: Pray for the blood of Jesus to cancel any lingering covenants.
- Reject false identities: Many Greek organizations assign titles, nicknames, or roles that become part of a person's identity. Renounce those and reaffirm your identity in Christ.
- Close the door to spiritual influence: Command any demonic spirits tied to those oaths, rituals, or organizations to leave in Jesus' name. According to James 4:17 (NIV): *"If anyone, then, knows the good they ought to do and doesn't do it, it is sin for them."*
- Dedicate yourself anew to God: Pray a prayer of surrender, declaring loyalty to Christ alone.

Ongoing Steps
- Accountability: Let a trusted pastor or Christian mentor know about your decision.
- Discipleship: Stay rooted in prayer, Scripture, and fellowship with other Christian believers.
- Replace the community: Many people join fraternities/sororities for a sense of belonging and social connection. Replace the Greek activities with church attendance, small group participation, and healthy Christian fellowship. If you don't know a group of Christian believers in your area, start one and put the word out! Do fun things together! There is life and vibrancy found in Christ.

Prayer: "Jesus, [Fraternity/Sorority Name] has been an important part of my life, but I am learning that the origin of it and many of its practices do not please you. Help me understand what you are asking me to do about my involvement in the fraternity/sorority. Give me the humility and boldness to quickly obey. Let my obedience open the door to more of You and the things you desire for me. Thank you for filling the places where the fraternity/sorority used to be with much better things. I trust you, and I ask these things by faith in Jesus' name, amen."

Promise Scriptures:
"If you love me, keep my commands." (John 14:15, NIV)

"Whoever has my commands and keeps them is the one who loves me. The one who loves me will be loved by my Father, and I too will love them and show myself to them." (John 14:21, NIV)

Chapter 3: Freemasonry

If you've ever driven past a building with a strange square-and-compass symbol or a big letter "G" in the middle, you've probably passed a Masonic lodge.

Freemasonry is one of the world's oldest and most secretive fraternal organizations. At its surface, Freemasonry presents itself as a brotherhood built on moral values, personal growth, and community service. Members refer to each other as "brothers," meet in lodges, perform rituals, and move through a series of degrees (or levels) of initiation. To many, Freemasonry appears harmless, like a club for networking, doing good deeds, and building character. But if you peel back the layers, you will find that Freemasonry is a far more spiritual organization than it is social, and that's where the concern begins.

To give you a bit of history, Freemasonry traces its roots back to the stonemasons of medieval Europe – the craftsmen who built cathedrals and castles. Over time, it evolved from an actual trade guild into a philosophical society that blended Enlightenment ideas, mystical symbolism, and ancient religious concepts. By the late 1500s, some lodges began admitting "speculative" members (non-working masons) who used the craft's symbols in a moral and philosophical way. On June 24, 1717, four London lodges formed the Grand Lodge of England, marking the beginning of organized Freemasonry as a worldwide fraternity.

Freemasonry spread widely across Europe and America, attracting influential leaders, politicians, and thinkers – including some who shaped the early United States. Freemasonry arrived in the American colonies by the 1730s. Many Founding Fathers of America – including George Washington and Benjamin Franklin – were Freemasons.

By the 18th Century, the three primary degrees (levels/steps) of Freemasonry were standardized: Entered Apprentice, Fellow Craft, and Master Mason. However, it is said there are 33 degrees in total. Some symbols of Freemasonry include the square and compasses, the letter "G" (supposedly for God/Geometry), and others. The symbols were adopted to teach moral lessons. However, as time progressed, the Freemasons began to add spiritual beliefs and principles to their practices.

Today, there are an estimated six million Freemasons worldwide, with the United States having the largest membership. There are men-only lodges, women's orders (Order of the Eastern Star), and youth branches (DeMolay and Job's Daughters). Members take oaths of secrecy, memorize rituals, and use symbolic language drawn from ancient temples, geometry, and spiritual storytelling.

While Masons often claim they're not a religion, their teachings borrow from many religious and occult systems, including Gnosticism (a religious movement that emphasizes secret knowledge as the key to salvation), Kabbalah (an ancient mystical tradition that seeks to explore the divine and the universe), and even Egyptian mystery cults. Freemasonry requires belief in a "Supreme Being," but not the God of the Bible. In fact, members are told that all religions lead to the same truth – a belief that directly contradicts John 14:6 (NIV) where Jesus said:

"I am the way and the truth and the life. No one comes to the Father except through me."'

In 1 Timothy 2:5-6a (NIV), it says:

"For there is one God and one mediator between God and mankind, the man Christ Jesus, who gave himself as a ransom for all people."

That's the key issue for Christians: Freemasonry replaces worship of the one true God with a system of symbols, secrecy, and self-enlightenment. Candidates must profess belief in a Supreme Being, though masonry itself is not considered a religion by its leaders. Lodges supposedly tend to focus on philanthropy, community service, social bonds, and personal development. However, opponents (especially many Christians) critique the use of secret oaths and obligations; the use of religious language without allegiance to Christ; and syncretism (the blending of faith traditions). In Freemasonry, God is referred to as the "Great Architect of the Universe (GAOTU)" – something that is deliberately vague so that people of any religion (Christian, Muslim, Hindu, etc.) can participate. This syncretism goes against the exclusive worship of the God of the Bible – the Father of Abraham, Isaac, and Jacob. Freemasonry never acknowledges Jesus Christ as Savior and the only way to the Father. Rather, masons are told they can gain moral enlightenment and a pathway to heaven through good works, rituals, and personal growth. Masons are also taught that they can reach higher moral and spiritual states by progressing through the three degrees mentioned earlier. On the contrary, the Bible clearly tells us about salvation through faith in Christ's finished work alone – that is, through Christ's death, burial, and resurrection on behalf of sinful mankind.

"For it is by grace you have been saved, through faith – and this is not from yourselves, it is the gift

of God – not by works, so that no one can boast."
(Ephesians 2:8-9, NIV)

Masons swear oaths of secrecy at each degree, often invoking curses on themselves if they break them. Jesus explicitly forbids this kind of oath-taking as we saw in Matthew 5:34-37.

Freemasonry uses symbols (all-seeing eye, compasses, pillars, etc.) with worldly spiritual meanings drawn from ancient mystery religions, not the Bible. Initiation ceremonies often mirror pagan death and rebirth rituals, symbolically guiding members toward "enlightenment". As we read in Deuteronomy 18:9-14, God forbids occult practices of any kind.

As you can see by what we've read in this chapter, anyone involved in Freemasonry ought to truly examine their allegiances if they want to honor and serve God. Come out of secrecy and into the light! Revoke and walk away from those ungodly oaths and serve the Lord Jesus Christ free and clear!

> *"Stand fast therefore in the liberty wherewith Christ hath made us free, and be not entangled again with the yoke of bondage." (Galatians 5:1, KJV)*

The true God is one with the Lord Jesus Christ and the Holy Spirit. Anyone else is a counterfeit.

> *"I am the Lord, and there is no other; apart from me there is no God." (Isaiah 45:5a, NIV)*

Call to Action: Follow the Call to Action at the end of Chapter 2 on Fraternities and Sororities.

Prayer: Pray the Prayer at the end of Chapter 2 on Fraternities and Sororities.

Promise Scripture:

"If we say that we have fellowship with him, and walk in darkness, we lie, and do not the truth: But if we walk in the light, as he is in the light, we have fellowship one with another, and the blood of Jesus Christ his Son cleanseth us from all sin. If we say that we have no sin, we deceive ourselves, and the truth is not in us. If we confess our sins, he is faithful and just to forgive us our sins, and to cleanse us from all unrighteousness. If we say that we have not sinned, we make him a liar, and his word is not in us." (1 John 1:6-10, KJV)

Chapter 4: Communicating with Ancestors and the Dead

"Do not turn to mediums or seek out spiritists, for you will be defiled by them. I am the Lord your God." (Leviticus 19:31, NIV)

My grandmother was someone I cherished very much. She was the kind of person who always listened, never judged (at least externally where I ever experienced it), and often sent you home with a parting gift after visiting her place – even if it was something as simple as an ice cream bar or a free copy of a daily devotional she received in the mail. I always felt at ease, loved, and welcome in her presence.

When I married my husband in August 2008, my grandmother was front and center at the wedding. The following year, I found out I was pregnant with our first child! I drove to my grandmother's place which was less than 10 minutes from my home to tell her the good news. We sat down at her small dinette set, and I broke the news that I was having a baby. She smiled and expressed her happiness for my husband and me, and took a guess that I was having a boy. We sat there and talked about what it would be like for me to be a mom.

A few weeks later, I called my grandmother after one of my prenatal checkups to tell her how it went, but she didn't answer the phone. I got the strangest feeling when she didn't answer, but brushed it away – thinking I was being too sensitive or that I was making a big deal out of nothing. I went home to continue my evening, and night turned into the next day.

My phone rang early the next morning, which was out of the ordinary because of the time. It was my mother. My spirit knew something was wrong, but I didn't allow myself to consider it. When I answered, my mother said my grandmother hadn't answered the phone when she called that morning. My grandmother was supposed to babysit my brother, as his regular babysitter had the day off and my mother had to go to work. My suspicion that something was wrong grew at that moment, because it was unlike my grandmother not to answer the phone, and she had now missed calls from both my mom and me. (Also, my grandmother, frankly, didn't have much of a social calendar, so I knew she wasn't out doing something else at that time of the morning, but I still didn't allow myself to face the truth.) My mother said she would have my grandmother's building send someone to her unit to perform a welfare check. At the same time, my mother began driving to my grandmother's building to see what was happening. The entire time, I waited at home because I didn't want to face the truth. I couldn't bring myself to consider it.

A little while later, my mother called back. I knew when I answered the phone that I was either going to receive news that my grandmother was fine and had simply been asleep, or that she had passed away. When I answered the phone, all suspicion was completely erased. My mother was crying and saying in a loud voice, "She's gone, Sabrina! She's gone." I went numb and didn't know what to do. My feelings had been right. My grandmother was gone. We were just talking about my baby only a few weeks before, and she seemed fine! But it was true. Just like that, my grandmother's spirit was no longer here on earth.

Of course, I went through the whole "What if?" routine. "What if I had gone straight to her house when she hadn't answered the previous afternoon? What if that feeling was trying to tell me something, and I ignored it? What if? What if? What if?" But the Lord didn't allow me to stay in that place too long. He knew it would have done me no good whatsoever.

When you love someone and they pass away, the ache of their absence can cause a myriad of thoughts, feelings, and even a sense of tangible, physical pain. That pain is very real, and even Jesus understood it. That is why the Bible says Jesus wept at the tomb of His friend Lazarus according to John Chapter 11. Jesus knows the sting of death, and He understood quite well when He encountered the news of Lazarus' death that His own death on the cross was a short time away.

Missing someone makes you want to do everything you can to hold onto them. You can still smell their scent in their clothing and sort of feel their presence in their home. Out of the pain of loss, it is easy to begin rationalizing ways to keep your loved one as near as possible.

After someone they love passes away, some people say things like, "Grandma always knew what to do, so I'll ask her for guidance." Or, "When I couldn't find my keys, I sent up a prayer to my friend Kyle to tell me where they were, and the curtains rustled in the dining room. The keys were on the table right next to the window. Thanks for always looking down on me!"

While those kinds of things sound sweet and encouraging – especially when you're missing someone – the reality is you should never consult the dead for advice.

> *"When someone tells you to consult mediums and spiritists, who whisper and mutter, should not a people inquire of their God? Why consult the dead on behalf of the living?" (Isaiah 8:19, NIV)*

Such activity opens the door to spiritual activity you would want no parts of. A trick of the enemy is convincing you that you can (or should) reach out to the dead for comfort or guidance. The Bible has a name for that: necromancy.

Necromancy, simply put, is the practice of communicating with the dead. In ancient times, it meant consulting mediums, spiritists, or witches who claimed they could "summon" the dead. Some people still do those things today, but necromancy can also look like:

- Going to psychics.
- Playing with Ouija boards or tarot cards.
- Pouring out drinks for deceased loved ones.
- Leaving food and drinks out for ancestors or deities.
- Watching popular shows where mediums "talk to dead loved ones" on behalf of those who remain here on earth and miss the deceased person terribly.

These kinds of practices have been around for a long time. The Egyptians built pyramids stuffed with goodies for their pharaohs so the dead would help the living. The Romans kept shrines in their homes where they talked to their ancestors. In Africa, Asia, and the Americas, ancestor veneration was (and in many places, still is) a major part of religion and culture. Pouring out drinks in many cultures is a way to communicate with the spirits of the dead and seek their guidance. Even the Bible gives us a famous case: King Saul and the Witch of Endor in 1 Samuel Chapter 28. King Saul was feeling desperate because the Lord had departed from him due to his disobedience, and he found himself in a situation. Not knowing what to do, the king consulted a medium who called up the prophet Samuel WHO WAS ALREADY DEAD! (It didn't end well. Everything that God said would happen to Saul, happened, and it wasn't good.)

It may seem harmless or even comforting to try and talk with a loved one from the great beyond, but such practices are a direct violation of God's Word as we read in multiple Scriptures in previous chapters. (See again Leviticus 19:31, Isaiah 8:19, Deuteronomy 18:9-14, and Galatians 5:19-21.) God calls witchcraft and similar practices detestable because He wants to be your source of comfort and information. Seeking guidance from and communication with the dead is wrongly taking matters into your own hands because of your pain. God wants to be your source of comfort and strength, and He does not want you to be deceived or open to other spirits by seeking out the dead.

If you miss your loved one and it seems to be too heavy for you to bear, here are a few steps you can take:

- Talk with friends, family members, and people you KNOW love you, as they will listen compassionately and allow you to share your heart. You are not burdening anyone. You are reaching out for the kind of help you would surely give someone else if the roles were reversed. It doesn't matter whether they have been through the same thing. Their love will help carry you through.
- Seek out a Christian grief counselor, as they can help you navigate this difficult time in your life. Seeking help from a trained professional to sort out complex thoughts and feelings is not unbiblical or un-Christian. It is no different from going to see the dentist for a toothache, or a doctor for a physical issue.
- Purposely engage in activities that bring you joy, even if it feels a bit weird at first. Do you like dancing? Start boogieing, even if it's an act of faith at first. Do you like working on cars? Break out those tools and get to tinkering!
- Find community in a Christian church or small group you know is a safe place. Ask God to lead you to a healthy, loving, and Bible-based place where you can get connected.

God has too many plans for your life for you to waste away. Do not let the enemy beat you down and keep you in depression. This may feel like a fight for your emotions and mind, but indeed, you are already the winner with Christ! Tap into the Bible, your church, and your loved ones. Fight back with the promises of God! You will absolutely win every time if you <u>intentionally</u> seek the joy of living again and DO NOT QUIT!

Call to Action:
In addition to the suggestions listed in this chapter for handling grief, if you've been involved in ancestral rituals or necromancy in any way, replace conversations with the dead with prayers to the Living God. You don't need to be involved with seeking the dead any longer – especially now that you know it is unnecessary and an offense to God. Renounce those practices and give Jesus full authority over your spiritual life. Ask God to replace those false comforts with real comfort from the Holy Spirit. Seek God, and He will surely be found by you. I say to you again: **DO NOT QUIT!**

Prayer for Those Who Have Participated in Necromancy: Lord Jesus, I confess that I have sought comfort, guidance, or connection by reaching out to the dead. I now understand that this is against Your Word. I repent and renounce every practice of necromancy, ancestor worship, and spirit communication I have participated in. I close every door I opened to the enemy, and I ask You to wash me clean with Your blood. Fill me with Your Holy Spirit, and remind me daily that You are the lover of my soul, comforter, and guide. I declare that my hope is in You alone. In Jesus' name I pray, amen.

Prayer for Those Who Are Having Difficulty with Grief and Loss: Lord, I have been struggling because [Name] passed away. I don't want to struggle, and I know you don't want me to be this way. You still have plans for my life, and I want you to fulfill them. Help me come out of this place of darkness. Lead me to the right people to help me through this phase of my life. I will not give up. Instead, I'm going to reach out to you and people who love me for help, and I will make it through this! I will purposely move to find life, peace, and joy again. I trust you to lead me, so I release my hold on [Name], and I grab hold of your love, your presence, and the people you have here on earth for me to enjoy and to help. And if I have moments of sorrow, help them not to overtake me the way they used to. I will not turn to ungodly or unhealthy crutches to make it through this. Instead, I will move forward confidently in your love and protection. I pray this in the mighty name of Jesus Christ my Lord, amen.

Promise Scriptures:
"The Lord is close to the brokenhearted and saves those who are crushed in spirit." (Psalm 34:18, NIV)

"But the Advocate, the Holy Spirit, whom the Father will send in my name, will teach you all things and will remind you of everything I have said to you." (John 14:26, NIV)

". . . Never will I leave you, never will I forsake you." (Hebrews 13:5b, NIV).

"Call to me and I will answer you and tell you great and unsearchable things you do not know." (Jeremiah 33:3, NIV)

(By the way, my grandmother's guess about my baby's gender was wrong. ☺ I had a girl first, followed by a boy two years later.)

Chapter 5: Crystals, Charms, Sage, and the Like

"Who changed the truth of God into a lie, and worshipped and served the creature more than the Creator, who is blessed for ever. Amen." (Romans 1:25, KJV)

The enemy is tricky. He does not show up in your life wearing horns and holding a pitchfork like in books and movies. Rather, he shows up in ways that seem harmless – even beautiful – like with a beautiful stone that promises peace and protection, or a candle labeled "prosperity" or "healing." But behind the marketing, sparkles, and lovely smells lies the same old lie: that you can find power, protection, and peace apart from God through objects <u>He</u> created.

Crystals, charms, and cleansing rituals like burning sage are part of an ancient spiritual system – one that teaches people to place faith in created things rather than the Creator. And while some people see them as harmless "energy tools," these practices trace their roots back to paganism, witchcraft, and idol worship – all of which God clearly condemns in His Word.

Let's be clear: Stones and plants have no spiritual power to heal your broken heart, cleanse your home, or protect your soul. Only God can do that. So, in this chapter, we're going to dig into how these practices originated, why they're so popular today, and what the Bible says about trusting in spiritual tools that were never meant to take God's place.

Do you know where the word "crystal" comes from? It stems from the Greek word "krystallos", meaning "clear ice." Greek and Roman cultures thought clear quartz was eternal ice sent from the heavens. Greeks also believed the amethyst kept you from getting drunk. In Ancient Mesopotamia and Egypt, crystals like lapis lazuli and turquoise were carved into amulets believed to protect against evil spirits. Egyptians buried their dead with crystals to "guide" them into the afterlife. In Medieval Europe, people wore gemstones in attempts to ward off demons, sickness, or bad luck. Kings and queens had charms sewn into their clothing as supposed methods of protection. In Eastern religions like Hinduism and Buddhism, crystals are still used to align "chakras" (points of energy in the body) or to aid in meditation.

So, while the branding has changed ("positive vibes," "manifesting," and "energy work," for example), the root remains the same, and the practice does not align with God's Word. The use of crystals, charms, etc., has always been rooted in reliance on self, and is considered idolatry. The Bible is clear: our help, healing, and protection come from God alone.

To be clear, God certainly made crystals and precious stones, so they're not evil in and of themselves. Some stones are even mentioned in the Bible as elements for decoration or building! In Revelation Chapter 21, various kinds of stones were used to build the walls and foundation of the New Jerusalem. In Exodus Chapter 28, God commanded the high priest's breastplate to be made using 12 precious stones such as amethyst, topaz, onyx, jasper, and more. The stones represented the 12 tribes of Israel, not items to be used like the Infinity Stones in the Marvel Universe.

The thing to consider is this: God never told us to use crystals in any other manner except for what was outlined in His Word (for building or decoration, for example). The stones themselves are not bad. Rather, it is people's misuse of them that brings in the error.

A mark of the devil's character is to pervert (intentionally misuse) the original purpose of something. If I wore a tire on my head and called it a hat, I would be perverting the intended use of the tire. Or, if I took a bag of M&Ms to the grocery store and attempted to use the pieces of candy to pay for my broccoli and potatoes, I would be sorely disappointed when I left the store empty-handed.

A biblical example of misuse is the rebranding of the rainbow.

> *"And God said, 'This is the sign of the covenant I am making between me and you and every living creature with you, a covenant for all generations to come: I have set my rainbow in the clouds, and it will be the sign of the covenant between me and the earth. Whenever I bring clouds over the earth and the rainbow appears in the clouds, I will remember my covenant between me and you and all living creatures of every kind. Never again will the waters become a flood to destroy all life. Whenever the rainbow appears in the clouds, I will see it and remember the everlasting covenant between God and all living creatures of every kind on the earth.' So God said to Noah, 'This is the sign of the covenant I have established between me and all life on the earth.'" (Genesis 9:12-17, NIV)*

God's intention for the rainbow was to remind us of His covenant of love every time we saw it. Today, the rainbow is used to represent something different – a specific lifestyle agenda. When you see a rainbow today, what do you think of: God's love and promises toward you, or something else?

Other examples of perversion include taking the focus away from celebrating the death, burial and resurrection of Christ and placing it on bunnies, chocolate, and marshmallow peeps; or replacing focus on the birth of Christ with a chubby man in a red and white suit who clearly cannot fit down a chimney. The list goes on.

The devil's strategy has not changed. Because he can't be Number 1, he attempts to pull people into his ways by distorting the use of anything God created. The same is true today with people who use crystals, charms, and other objects. They take something God created and twist it into a use for which it was not intended.

Another common practice people have today is using sage in an effort to ward off evil spirits and "negative energy". Sage is actually a shrub from the mint family that is native to the Mediterranean, and is known for its distinctive aroma and savory, earthy flavor. People burn dried sage bundles and let the smoke spread through a room, over a person, or around objects in an attempt to "invite positive energy". Some also claim sage can drive away evil spirits or cleanse the soul before meditating or participating in various rituals. Sage is sometimes used before yoga classes or "energy healing" ceremonies to create a "purified, sacred space". Some use it to try and reset their environment to a place of peace – especially after an argument, illness, emotional distress, or a visit from someone whose attitude they don't prefer. In many Native American traditions, sage is considered a sacred plant, and is used in ceremonies to connect with ancestors or the spiritual world.

You may say, "But Sabrina, you don't know everything! If you traveled the world, you'd see that not everyone does everything the same as you! You have to be open to other ways of doing things, and understand that not everyone is westernized.

This kind of thinking is an issue because sage burning and the use of objects like crystals are essentially attempts to replace reliance on God with self-effort. Instead of asking the Lord for guidance, protection, cleansing, or whatever else is needed, people are essentially relying on smoke and special smells to protect and guide them. This is a major issue that must be addressed. If your peace comes from a physical rock instead of the Rock of Ages (God Himself), you are being deceived.

Scripture teaches us that only the blood of Jesus can cleanse us from sin:

"But if we walk in the light, as He is in the light, we have fellowship with one another, and the blood of Jesus, His Son, purifies us from all sin." (1 John 1:7, NIV)

You don't need sage, crystals, or any other created thing to keep you safe or cleanse you. You need the presence of God the Father, Jesus the Son, and the Holy Spirit in your life.

"I lift up my eyes to the mountains – where does my help come from? My help comes from the Lord, the Maker of heaven and earth. He will not let your foot slip – he who watches over you will not slumber; indeed, he who watches over Israel will neither slumber nor sleep. The Lord watches over you – the Lord is your shade at your right hand; the sun will not harm you by day, nor the moon by night. The Lord will keep you from all harm – he will watch over your life; the Lord will watch over your coming and going both now and forevermore." (Psalm 121, NIV)

Also, if you choose to read it, Psalm 91 provides an excellent outline regarding the protection of God.

In 2 Corinthians 11:14-15, the Bible describes Satan as one who disguises himself. Crystals, charms, and the use of sage are all forms of spiritual disguises. They are flashy and showy on the outside, but empty and devoid of power otherwise.

Let's end this chapter by looking at what you should do to rid your environment and heart of reliance on sage, crystals, and other ungodly tools.

Call to Action: If you've been dabbling with crystals, charms, and other such objects, it's time to ask yourself: "Do I want to trust God and His power, or something God created?" Get rid of the crystals, sage, and other objects you've been using for energy, healing, fortune, or anything else for favorable results. Don't trick yourself into keeping them for decoration or jewelry if you've already used them for ungodly purposes. Don't sell or give the items away, as that would be passing the problem along to someone else. Instead, throw away the objects or destroy them like the believers in Acts 19:19 who burned their magic scrolls. Ask Jesus to be your source of peace, protection, healing, wisdom, and power. Then fill your home, car, and space with prayer, worship, and the Word of God. God is faithful to His Word to take care of you. Dare to trust Him.

Prayer: "Father, I renounce my use of crystals, charms, sage, and any other object or plant for positive results. I break any ties I've made by trusting in these things instead of You. I declare that You alone are my peace, protector, healer, source of knowledge, and strength. I ask You to fill every place in my heart, home, and environment with Your Spirit. I thank you that every ungodly stone has been unturned, and your Spirit dwells where the enemy used to linger. I declare this in Jesus' name, amen."

Promise Scriptures:
"In you, Lord my God, I put my trust. I trust in you; do not let me be put to shame, nor let my enemies triumph over me. No one who hopes in you will ever be put to shame . . ." (Psalm 25:1-3a, NIV)

"Do not be anxious about anything, but in every situation, by prayer and petition, with thanksgiving, present your requests to God. And the peace of God, which transcends all understanding, will guard your hearts and your minds in Christ Jesus. (Philippians 4:6-7, NIV)

Chapter 6: Yoga, Mantras, and Chants

Yoga studios and classes are everywhere, and they are very popular. You can take all types of yoga classes these days, including goat yoga or puppy yoga where tiny animals climb all over you during the class in an attempt to make the whole thing innocent and sweet. But here is the truth: Yoga isn't just about stretching or exercising. It is actually a Hindu discipline that dates back thousands of years with very deep spiritual connotations.

We are going to break down what some of the most popular yoga poses really mean, and the actions you are symbolizing through the submission of your body when you do them. But before we do, let's look at the definition of the word "yoga".

The word "yoga" itself means "to yoke" or "to unite." An important question to ask yourself is, "When I'm doing yoga, what exactly am I yoking or uniting myself with?"

Yoga was designed as a way to yoke oneself to Hindu gods and pursue enlightenment. Each pose was (and still is) a form of worship to a deity. Let's look at a breakdown of what some of the most popular poses represent.

The Sun Salutation (Surya Namaskar) is one of the most popular yoga sequences of movements. Each movement is designed as an offering to the Hindu sun god, Surya. The bows, stretches, and hand positions are acts of reverence to Surya, a false god.

The Lotus Pose (Padmasana) is the cross-legged position often seen in meditation. It symbolizes lotus flowers rising above muddy water, meaning "spiritual enlightenment" or rising above the world. Spiritually speaking, it is meant to prepare the body as a throne for the spirit and awaken kundalini energy (a serpent-like power in Hinduism stemming from the base of the spine).

The Warrior Poses (Virabhadrasana I, II, III) are named after a mythical Hindu warrior, Virabhadra, created by the god Shiva. Practicing these poses is honoring that warrior and the violent story of his battles. Many people unknowingly "enact" this pagan story through their bodies.

Are you getting the picture now? Let's continue.

The Tree Pose (Vrikshasana) mimics standing like a rooted tree. It symbolizes being connected to the earth and drawing energy from it. The move promotes pantheistic thinking (the belief that God is in everything, including nature), which contradicts the Bible's clear teaching that God is separate from His creation.

The Cobra Pose (Bhujangasana) is part of a sequence known as the Sun Salutation. The pose represents a serpent rising – linked to the kundalini energy we read about as part of the Lotus pose. Christians know the serpent provides a picture of Satan, so why would we mimic that form in any manner?

Downward-Facing Dog (Adho Mukha Svanasana) is popular for stretching, but its original design is to mimic a submissive bowing position. It is rooted in honoring creation through animal forms, another example of drawing spiritual power from creation rather than the Creator.

The Corpse Pose (Savasana) is done lying flat on your back at the end of a yoga session. It symbolizes death and surrender – originally meant as a practice of "dying to self" so that one could be reborn into union with the Hindu concept of Brahman (the "universal spirit"). Many yoga classes use this as the final meditative point as a way of inviting students to "empty themselves for universal connection." Yikes.

Even if it was not your intent, do you now see how involving yourself in yoga gets you involved in a much deeper, darker spiritual practice that does not honor Jesus Christ as Lord?

"See to it that no one takes you captive through hollow and deceptive philosophy, which depends on human tradition and the elemental spiritual forces of this world rather than on Christ."
(Colossians 2:8, NIV)

Mantras are also a big part of yoga. The word "mantra" comes from Sanskrit. It is a combination of the word "man" (mind) and "tra" (instrument or tool). A mantra is essentially a "tool for the mind" – a repeated sound, word, or phrase used to focus attention and invoke spiritual energy.

You may not know that chanting mantras is meant to invoke deities. Each sound is believed to summon or honor a god. Chanting mantras is also meant to alter consciousness. Repetition is meant to create a trance-like state where the person is open to spiritual influences. Chanting is also meant to "manifest desires" such as health, wealth, and love.

In Hinduism and Buddhism, mantras are not just words. They are believed to carry power that connects the person chanting with a specific deity or cosmic force. In other words, mantras and chants were (are) considered prayers to false gods. Repeating them is not "empty mindfulness" – it is actually calling on spiritual powers that are not of Christ.

One of the most common mantras we've probably all heard with yoga is the "Om/Aum" sound. It is considered "the sacred sound of the universe" in Hinduism. Chanting it is said to connect you with "ultimate reality" (Brahman).

Other chants include:
- Om Namah Shivaya, which means, "I bow to Lord Shiva" (who is known as "the destroyer").
- So'ham (I am that), which declares "I am one with the universe" or "I am God".
- Gayatri Mantra, which is a chant directed to the sun god Savitar that is often recited for enlightenment and divine knowledge.
- Lokah Samastah Sukhino Bhavantu, which means, "May all beings everywhere be happy and free". This sounds nice, but it is rooted in the Hindu idea of karma and reincarnation rather than God's plan of salvation.

"I am the Lord, and there is no other; apart from me there is no God. I will strengthen you, though you have not acknowledged me." (Isaiah 45:5, NIV)

Social media promotes morning mantras and affirmations encouraging people to repeat phrases like "I am enough," "I am divine," or "I attract abundance." New Age circles use mantras as tools for "manifesting your best life," which places trust in repetition or the universe, not in God.

Consider these Scriptures as you think about whether yoga, chants, and mantras are okay to practice:

"Be careful to do everything I have said to you. Do not invoke the names of other gods; do not let them be heard on your lips." (Exodus 23:13, NIV)

"Death and life are in the power of the tongue: and they that love it shall eat the fruit thereof." (Proverbs 18:21, KJV)

"Out of the same mouth come praise and cursing. My brothers and sisters, this should not be." (James 3:10, NIV)

Instead of empty chants, God calls us to fill our mouths and minds with His Word and His praises:

"I will bless the Lord at all times: his praise shall continually be in my mouth." (Psalm 34:1, KJV)

"Let the words of my mouth, and the meditation of my heart, be acceptable in thy sight, O Lord, my strength, and my redeemer." (Psalm 19:14, KJV)

Again, I am not attempting to make everything a sin. God is not against you having peace, rest, or engaging in physical exercise. I am simply trying to uncover the root of some of these practices so you can choose for yourself whether you think it is right to continue.

"And if it seem evil unto you to serve the Lord, choose you this day whom ye will serve; whether the gods which your fathers served that were on the other side of the flood, or the gods of the Amorites, in whose land ye dwell: but as for me and my house, we will serve the Lord." (Joshua 24:15, KJV)

Let me tell you about something that happened to my mother very recently (in fact, while I was writing this book). She wanted to find exercise classes in her area as part of keeping herself healthy and active. She did some research and decided to enroll in several types of fitness classes over the span of three months. Water aerobics and line dancing were a few examples. My mom had also been seeing commercials on TV and social media for months advertising "chair yoga". While looking for classes in her area, she saw a chair yoga series of classes being advertised at a location very close to her home. It was the first time the class was being offered there. Although she had some hesitancy due to her knowledge of some of the practices of regular yoga, my mom reasoned that chair yoga might offer a regular form of exercise without any of the bells and whistles of regular yoga. As a result, she signed up to try the chair yoga class. What's funny is, as she was retelling the story to me, she explained she didn't tell me she was taking the class because she knew I would try talking her out of going. (She was right!)

My mother arrived at her first chair yoga class and assessed the room. Everything looked and seemed as normal as ever, and there were chairs set up for the class. When the session began, the instructor turned down the lights and began calmly explaining what to do. My mom was cautiously going along with the instructions and movements when the teacher told the participants to place their hands in the form of a tree. This raised my mom's spiritual antennas, but she said on the inside, "Uh, uh. Lord, I'm raising my hands to YOU!" (Hint: When you have to start reasoning why you're doing something, you already know something's wrong with it.)

As the class went on, the teacher lit incense and began burning sage. My mother's spiritual antennas were not just awakened at that point. They were heightened. (I'm almost laughing as I type this story, because I can see her in a room full of people doing yoga, but trying to act normal and not look alarmed.)

The teacher instructed the participants to place their hands in a praying motion in front of their chest. At that moment, my mother thought, "No, Jesus! I'm praying to YOU. The Father, Son, and Holy Spirit." At some point, the downward dog was instructed. The teacher kept referencing "the mind" and "the body" in ways that made my mom uncomfortable, but on she went! (And higher the spiritual antennas went, too.)

Then came the bell ringing. This almost brought my mother to a fever pitch! But what was really the straw that broke the camel's back was the instructor directing everyone to place their hands on their forehead, and referencing something about the "third eye". My mom said (and I quote), "Literally everything in me wanted to run out of that class! I was done!"

Once the class was over, she already knew she wasn't going back, and the next day called to request a refund for the remaining classes. I then shared with her what some of the poses represented, and she was horrified. (I'm laughing now because I'm recalling our conversation, but the reality of what she was doing is not funny at all!)

The point of sharing my mother's story (and this entire chapter) is that God doesn't want you yoking yourself to any evil thing or any other "god". He wants you to be happy, healthy, and holy, and those things are only found in Him through His Son, Jesus Christ.

> *"For in him we live, and move, and have our being . . ." (Acts 17:28a, KJV)*

> *But thanks be to God! He gives us the victory through our Lord Jesus Christ. (1 Corinthians 15:57, NIV)*

If you've been involved with yoga, mantras, and chants, it's time to take some specific actions, and then we'll pray.

Call to Action: Have you been using yoga as a form of exercise? Or have you been using yoga, mantras, or chants to seek peace or get results? Decide to renounce those practices right now – no matter what other people think. Stretch and exercise if you'd like, but don't tie your body or movements to the worship of another "god" or spirit. Purposely replace yoga with another form of exercise that is free of any ties to a foreign god. Replace mantras with Scriptures (the Word of God). Ask God to give you wisdom and spiritual discernment in your daily life (work, exercise, family, friends, love life, and anything else). God is faithful to answer and guide you.

Prayer: Heavenly Father, I repent for any way I have opened ungodly doors through yoga, mantras, chants, and other practices of Buddhism, Hinduism, the occult, and other non-Christlike influences. My desire is to serve the Lord Jesus Christ. In the name of Jesus, I break every yoke of bondage off my life. I renounce the chants and mantras I've spoken. I break ties to yoga in all forms. Lord, I choose Your way. Fill me with Your Holy Spirit. Help me to meditate on Your Word day and night, and to walk in Your truth. In Jesus' name I pray, amen.

Promise Scripture: *"For physical training is of some value, but godliness has value for all things, holding promise for both the present life and the life to come." (1 Timothy 4:8, NIV)*

"Thou wilt keep him in perfect peace, whose mind is stayed on thee: because he trusteth in thee." (Isaiah 26:3, KJV)

"Come to me, all you who are weary and burdened, and I will give you rest." (Matthew 11:28, NIV)

Chapter 7: Astrology and the Stars

"I'm sorry, but I'm not interested in your friend. He's a Leo."

"She acts just like her mother! That's that Capricorn energy."

If you've ever heard someone talk like this, or if you've been asked, "What's your sign?" then you know zodiac and astrology are quite commonplace today.

There is a show on YouTube I love to watch. I've watched it often enough that my husband and daughter now watch the show with me sometimes. (My teenage son? Not so much.) The premise of the show is that a lineup of single people holding inflated balloons and looking for love is introduced to other singles one by one. The lineup for each episode is either made up of all men or all women. If there is a lineup of women, single male contestants come out one at a time, introduce themselves, and begin asking questions of the women. If there is anything about the man that the women don't like – either because of looks, something he said, or any other reason – the women can pop their balloon. This signifies they are no longer interested in that contestant. Some of the contestants leave with a match. Others do not.

In addition to questions about faith, career, finances, and other important topics, a question that is sometimes asked by a contestant is, "What's your sign?" If the contestant gives the wrong answer, they are often rejected because, "A Virgo hurt me in the past," or "My last boyfriend was a Taurus, and I will never date one again." My family and I always give each other a "not again" look and chuckle whenever we hear those kinds of comments, but some people really base life and love decisions based on zodiac signs.

Astrology dates back thousands of years to ancient Babylon. The Babylonians believed the stars and planets controlled human destiny. They charted the skies and created zodiac signs based on constellations. By the time of the Greeks and Romans, astrology had been fused into the philosophical and religious arenas. Kings and emperors often had court astrologers who advised them on war, politics, and daily decisions.

The Bible speaks directly about the topic of astrology. Here is just one of those Scriptures:

> *"All the counsel you have received has only worn you out! Let your astrologers come forward, those stargazers who make predictions month by month, let them save you from what is coming upon you."* (Isaiah 47:13, NIV)

God is basically saying, "Ask your stargazers for help. Let's see if they can save you when disaster comes."

The zodiac wasn't invented as a harmless, fun activity; nor should it be considered as a guide for anyone who wants to honor God. Rather, zodiac and astrology are tied to false gods and myths that directly compete with the worship of the One True God. Here is a quick overview:

- Aries (The Ram): Linked to Ares, the war god.
- Taurus (The Bull): Fertility idol. Recall Israel's golden calf in Exodus 32.
- Gemini (The Twins): Tied to Castor and Pollux, prayed to by sailors.
- Cancer (The Crab): From Greek myths, symbol of cycles.
- Leo (The Lion): Symbol of kingship and power, worshipped in Babylon.
- Virgo (The Virgin): Connected to fertility goddesses like Ishtar.
- Libra (The Scales): Associated with Astraea, goddess of law and justice.

- Scorpio (The Scorpion): Linked to mystery, death, and hidden wisdom.
- Sagittarius (The Archer): Connected to Chiron the centaur.
- Capricorn (The Goat): Hybrid goat-fish symbol of the god Enki.
- Aquarius (The Water Bearer): Linked to the gods of floods and water.
- Pisces (The Fish): Associated with Aphrodite and Eros.

Each sign tied people's identity and destiny to false gods rather than God the Father.

Astrology often slips under the radar because it seems "less intense" than the use of physical objects or performing physical actions. But at its core, astrology is idolatry. It says, "Don't look to God for direction. Look to elements created by God for answers."

The Bible is crystal clear about this:

> *"And when you look up to the sky and see the sun, the moon and the stars – all the heavenly array – do not be enticed into bowing down to them and worshiping things the Lord your God has apportioned to all the nations under heaven." (Deuteronomy 4:19, NIV)*

> *"Thus saith the Lord, Learn not the way of the heathen, and be not dismayed at the signs of heaven; for the heathen are dismayed at them." (Jeremiah 10:2, KJV)*

At its very root, astrology replaces trust in God by attempting to know and control outcomes. Instead of leaning on the Creator, people lean on constellations and objects that cannot hear, speak, or move in a godly way on their behalf. A better way for people who want to honor God can be found in the Scriptures:

"Trust in the Lord with all thine heart; and lean not unto thine own understanding. In all thy ways acknowledge him, and he shall direct thy paths." (Proverbs 3:5-6, KJV)

"If any of you lacks wisdom, you should ask God, who gives generously to all without finding fault, and it will be given to you." (James 1:5, NIV)

The stars were created to point us to the Creator, not replace Him. The sun was created for everyone to benefit from its light and heat, not to be worshipped or consulted. The moon was created to help rule the tides and to cast its light at night, not to be worshipped or created.

Here are some reasons why astrology is spiritually dangerous for anyone, but particularly for Christians:

1. It promotes identity outside of Christ.
Astrology teaches that who you are is shaped by your zodiac sign, not by being made in the image of God. (See Genesis 1:27.)

2. It leads people to depend on created things for guidance.
Astrology teaches that stars control your destiny. But Scripture teaches the opposite as we read in Chapter 5:

"My help comes from the Lord, the Maker of heaven and earth." (Psalm 121:2, NIV)

3. It opens doors to divination and deception.
Astrology is a form of divination, which God repeatedly condemns as we read in Deuteronomy 18:9-14. Consulting horoscopes, star charts, birth alignments, and other astrological tools invites spiritual influences that are not from God.

4. It subtly replaces God with "the universe."

Many forms of astrology refer to "the universe" granting favor or providing guidance. This shifts people from honoring God as their source and provider to something vague or some kind of cosmic force. This is idolatry.

5. It becomes an excuse for sin.

Zodiac's logic often justifies ungodly behavior: "I'm rude because I'm an Aries," "I get angry because I'm a Scorpio," etc. Instead of confession and repentance, astrology gives people an excuse to act any way they please because, "It's just how my sign acts."

Many former astrologers testify that dependence on astrological tools led them into anxiety, depression, and spiritual darkness. Other people who began with simple horoscopes or palm readings for guidance eventually became dependent on those tools and later experienced deep fear, nightmares, and demonic oppression until they renounced astrology altogether.

As we read in 2 Corinthians 5:17, we become new creations when we are in Christ. You aren't the same old person you were before! God gives you a new identity through His Son. That identity has nothing to do with stars, symbols, or your zodiac sign. Therefore, it's time to renounce those things and walk fully in who God made you to be.

Call to Action: If you've been relying on horoscopes, zodiac signs, or astrology in any manner, or if you've been referencing them as part of your regular conversation, it's time to do something different. Delete any astrology apps. Toss the zodiac books and guides. Remove those things from your space and your conversations. Stop asking the stars for what only the Creator of the stars can give you. Choose to go to God for wisdom, direction, and comfort. He won't let you down when you trust Him.

Prayer: Heavenly Father, I repent for any way I've looked to or referenced astrology, horoscopes, or the stars for guidance. Forgive me for replacing your voice, your Word, and your presence with false voices. I renounce every word I've spoken in agreement with those practices, and I break off their influence from my life in the name of Jesus. Lord, help me to trust You alone with my past, present, and future. Teach me to hear Your voice clearly and not follow another. Because of what Jesus did for me on the cross, I thank You that my name is written in the Lamb's Book of Life. I pray this in Jesus' name, amen.

Promise Scripture: *"If my people, which are called by my name, shall humble themselves, and pray, and seek my face, and turn from their wicked ways; then will I hear from heaven, and will forgive their sin, and will heal their land." (2 Chronicles 7:14, KJV)*

Chapter 8: Manifesting, Law of Attraction, and Ungodly Meditation

Manifesting and the Law of Attraction are widely referenced practices, and are even accepted and utilized in Christian circles. Those practices suggest that, if you think positive thoughts repeatedly enough, or confess the right words long enough, "the universe" will hand-deliver your desires to your doorstep like an Amazon Prime package.

I want you to notice something very key: The difference in manifesting and the Bible kind of speaking is subtle on the surface, but it's glaring when you look deeper. Manifesting focuses on <u>you</u> repeatedly saying or doing something to get <u>your</u> desired result (acting in your own strength) – often without first consulting God. On the other hand, speaking the Word of God and His promises focuses on <u>God and His faithfulness</u> based on His character and <u>what He has already spoken</u>. One trusts in <u>your</u> ability to babble over and over; the other trusts in God's love and power to act on your behalf based on His character and who He is.

"But Sabrina, the Bible says that faith without works is dead according to James Chapter 2. And there is a scripture in Proverbs 23:7a (KJV) that says:

"For as he thinketh in his heart, so is he . . ."

The key questions are: In what are you placing your faith, and what are you confessing? In other words, if you are focusing on your ability to repeatedly confess something (outside of Scripture) until the desired result comes, your faith is not in God. It is in yourself. Are you focusing on a promise you can back up with Scripture from God's Word, or perhaps a prophecy from a trusted Christian vessel that confirmed something God had already spoken to you? Or are you focusing on something (or someone) you've set your eyes upon and decided to begin confessing for it simply because you want it? It is of the utmost importance that you inquire of God before pursuing things in this life. The will of God should be the source of your actions rather than you picking something for yourself and trying to get God to co-sign. If you're not sure what God's will is, as we read in James Chapter 1 earlier in this book, you can simply ask God for wisdom, and He will give it to you!

Manifesting and the Law of Attraction are cousins. They are born from the MeMe Family tree. That is, "I'M manifesting this. I'M manifesting that. I'M attracting this into my life." That kind of speaking is not rooted in God. Rather, it is ungodly self-reliance, idolatry, and witchcraft. If you don't believe me, let's look deeper.

The Law of Attraction was popularized by a book called *The Secret*, published in 2006, and is basically a modern rebranding of the New Thought Movement that began in the mid-to-late 1800s (a movement that was influenced by mesmerism (hypnosis), spiritualism, Transcendentalism, Hinduism, and metaphysical philosophy). While many Christian believers have sung the praises of that book, its roots are not in line with Biblical teaching because it shifts the focus away from God as the source of life and blessing to self as the source. It also denies sin, and instead claims people only suffer because of "wrong thinking." The Bible clearly says:

"For all have sinned and fall short of the glory of God."
(Romans 3:23, NIV)

"If we say that we have no sin, we deceive ourselves, and the truth is not in us." (1 John 1:8, KJV)

New Thought and the Law of Attraction teach us to consult with ourselves to find the answers we need. The Bible teaches:

"Do not conform to the pattern of this world, but be transformed by the renewing of your mind. Then you will be able to test and approve what God's will is— his good, pleasing and perfect will." (Romans 12:2, NIV)

New Thought teaches, "You are divine." The Bible teaches:

"Hear, O Israel: The Lord our God is one Lord." (Deuteronomy 6:4, KJV)

"I am the vine; you are the branches. If you remain in me and I in you, you will bear much fruit; apart from me you can do nothing." (John 15:5, NIV)

"For I know the plans I have for you," declares the Lord, "plans to prosper you and not to harm you, plans to give you hope and a future." (Jeremiah 29:11, NIV)

Ungodly meditation teaches people to empty their minds, repeat mantras, or visualize outcomes until circumstances bend to their desires. However, this is the kind of meditation the Bible speaks about:

"Keep this Book of the Law always on your lips; meditate on it day and night, so that you may be careful to do everything written in it. Then you will be prosperous and successful." (Joshua 1:8, NIV)

"This is what the Lord says: "Cursed is the one who trusts in man, who draws strength from mere flesh and whose heart turns away from the Lord. That

person will be like a bush in the wastelands; they
will not see prosperity when it comes.
They will dwell in the parched places of the
desert, in a salt land where no one lives. "But
blessed is the one who trusts in the Lord, whose
confidence is in him. They will be like a tree planted
by the water that sends out its roots by the stream. It
does not fear when heat comes; its leaves are always
green. It has no worries in a year of drought and
never fails to bear fruit." (Jeremiah 17:5-8, NIV)

In Matthew 26:39 (KJV), even Jesus Himself presented
His request to the Father, but ended with, "Nevertheless,
not as I will, but as thou wilt." Jesus didn't repeat the
same words over and over to get his way. Instead, He
went to God, presented His heart, and asked that God's
will be done. He then went forward in what He knew was
God's will.

If you are not sure what God's will is in a matter, you are
free to keep seeking Him until you do.

"Ask, and it shall be given you; seek, and ye shall
find; knock, and it shall be opened unto you: For
every one that asketh receiveth; and he that seeketh
findeth; and to him that knocketh it shall be opened.
Or what man is there of you, whom if his son ask
bread, will he give him a stone? Or if he ask a fish,
will he give him a serpent? If ye then, being evil,
know how to give good gifts unto your children, how
much more shall your Father which is in heaven
give good things to them that ask him?" (Matthew
7:7-11, KJV)

"A man's heart deviseth his way: but
the Lord directeth his steps." (Proverbs 16:9, KJV)

"Every good and perfect gift is from above, coming
down from the Father of the heavenly lights, who

does not change like shifting shadows. (James 1:17, NIV)

"Blessed is the one who does not walk in step with the wicked or stand in the way that sinners take or sit in the company of mockers, but whose delight is in the law of the Lord, and who meditates on his law day and night. That person is like a tree planted by streams of water, which yields its fruit in season and whose leaf does not wither – whatever they do prospers." (Psalm 1:1-3, NIV)

Here is a comparison chart that will help you see the difference between ungodly and Godly meditating:

	Worldly Meditation	Godly/Biblical Meditation
Focus	Self, thoughts, feelings, the universe, or inner peace	God, His Word, His character, His works
References	Affirmations, visualizations, mantras, chants, breathing exercises	Scripture, prayer, thanksgiving, pondering God's truth
Goal/ Purpose	Emotional calm, enlightenment, receiving one's own personal desires	Spiritual growth, discernment, intimacy with God, obedience
Method	Emptying or controlling the mind; self-direction, repetition of ungodly phrases, ungodly introspection	Filling the mind with God's Word; guided by the Holy Spirit; reading and acting according to God's Word
Outcome	Temporary peace or insight in some instances, but can lead to deception, confusion, and ungodly results	Godly transformation of heart and mind; wisdom; peace; being rooted in God; practical, godly living

As you have read, manifesting, the Law of Attraction, ungodly meditation, and similar practices are spiritual deceptions. They are human attempts to decide what is best for your own life and "declare it into existence". Unless your confessions are backed by properly-applied Scripture, or what God has confirmed to you through a trusted Christian vessel, you should check them very carefully.

If you discover you have been participating in manifesting, the Law of Attraction, or ungodly meditation, there are specific actions I'd invite you to take.

Call to Action:
There is a difference between self-reliance and God-reliance. God wants you to seek and put your trust in Him rather than setting your sights on something and babbling endlessly to get it. Replace ungodly meditation and random speaking with ongoing contemplation about God's Word and His promises. Ask God what His will is for the various areas of your life. Your Heavenly Father loves you and knows what you need before you ask. He will show you what to declare over your life – even from His Word.

Prayer:
Heavenly Father, I confess that I have tried to control parts of my life apart from You. I renounce any involvement with manifesting, the Law of Attraction, and ungodly meditation. Forgive me for trusting in the universe or in my own repeated words instead of Your promises. I declare that You alone are my Provider, Guide, and Source. Help me to meditate on Your Word day and night, trust in Your perfect plan, and walk by faith in Jesus Christ rather than only what I can see. It's in Jesus' name I pray, amen.

Promise Scripture: *"But when you pray, go into your room, close the door and pray to your Father, who is unseen. Then your Father, who sees what is done in secret, will reward you. And when you pray, do not keep on babbling like pagans, for they think they will be heard because of their many words. Do not be like them, for your Father knows what you need before you ask him."* *(Matthew 6:6-8, NIV)*

Chapter 9: Now What?

If you've reached this point in the book, you've walked through what were potentially some hard truths – truths about witchcraft, rebellion, and spiritual counterfeits that have quietly crept into modern-day life. Perhaps you or someone you love has practiced some of the things you've read about because you didn't know what they were really about until now.

If you have recognized yourself in any chapter within this book, know that God's conviction is never meant to shame you. Rather, it is meant to warn and rescue you from danger and error. God's correction comes out of His great love for you. Someone who loves you would never want you to remain in a compromising situation.

Throughout this book, you've seen how the enemy tends to repackage sin (witchcraft, idolatry, and rebellion) as "self-care," "spirituality," or "personal growth." While it is perfectly healthy (and encouraged) for you to work, exercise, and engage in God-given relationships, it is not meant for you to engage in witchcraft. You cannot mix light and darkness and expect to honor God or walk in His best for your life.

> *"Do not be yoked together with unbelievers. For what do righteousness and wickedness have in common? Or what fellowship can light have with darkness?"*
> *(2 Corinthians 6:14, NIV)*

God is calling His people to come out from the evil things and be separate. We must vow to stop dabbling in what God has clearly called detestable, because we know He would never steer us wrong. He always has our best interests at heart.

If a particular chapter of this book hit home for you (or maybe made you say, "Ouch!"), I'd encourage you to review that chapter again – especially the Call to Action, Prayer, and Promise Scripture(s). God is not attempting to take something away to deprive or punish you. He's asking you to honor Him by living in a way that will bring life to you and others.

The Blessing of Obedience
When you choose to obey God, you are stepping into blessing.

"If you are willing and obedient, you will eat the good things of the land." (Isaiah 1:19, NIV)

"All these blessings will come on you and accompany you if you obey the Lord your God: You will be blessed in the city and blessed in the country. The fruit of your womb will be blessed, and the crops of your land and the young of your livestock – the calves of your herds and the lambs of your flocks. Your basket and your kneading trough will be blessed. You will be blessed when you come in and blessed when you go out. The Lord will grant that the enemies who rise up against you will be defeated before you. They will come at you from one direction but flee from you in seven. The Lord will send a blessing on your barns and on everything you put your hand to. The Lord your God will bless you in the land he is giving you. The Lord will establish you as his holy people, as he promised you on oath, if you keep the commands of the Lord your God and walk in obedience to him. Then all the peoples on earth will see that you are called by the name of the Lord, and they will fear you. The Lord will grant you abundant prosperity – in the fruit of your womb, the young of your livestock and the crops of your ground – in the land he swore to your ancestors to give you. The Lord will open the heavens, the

storehouse of his bounty, to send rain on your land
in season and to bless all the work of your hands.
You will lend to many nations but will borrow from
none. The Lord will make you the head, not the tail.
If you pay attention to the commands of
the Lord your God that I give you this day and
carefully follow them, you will always be at the top,
never at the bottom. Do not turn aside from any of
the commands I give you today, to the right or to the
left, following other gods and serving them."
(Deuteronomy 28:2-14, NIV)

Obedience to God sets you free from bondage and places
you on the path to freedom.

As you move forward, remember that any struggle with
witchcraft should be seen more as a spiritual one than a
physical one.

"Finally, be strong in the Lord and in his mighty
power. Put on the full armor of God, so that you can
take your stand against the devil's schemes. For our
struggle is not against flesh and blood, but against
the rulers, against the authorities, against the
powers of this dark world and against the spiritual
forces of evil in the heavenly realms. Therefore put
on the full armor of God, so that when the day of evil
comes, you may be able to stand your ground, and
after you have done everything, to stand."
(Ephesians 6:10-13, NIV)

"I write to you, dear children, because you know the
Father. I write to you, fathers, because you know
him who is from the beginning. I write to you, young
men, because you are strong, and the word of
God lives in you, and you have overcome the evil
one." (1 John 2:14, NIV)

*"Submit yourselves therefore to God. Resist the
devil, and he will flee from you." (James 4:7, KJV)*

A Final Word of Hope
No ritual, curse, or idol is stronger than the blood of Jesus.
The same Savior who broke death's hold can break any
chain in your life.

If you must leave something (or someone) behind, Jesus
will surely fill that void and add other good things and
people to your life over time. Try not to worry about what
you must leave behind. Trust me when I tell you: GOD
HAS BETTER! It makes me think of this popular picture
that has circulated online for a long time:

As you go forward, I encourage you to walk away from
ungodly choices and choose God's way – fully, freely, and
fearlessly!

Call to Action:
1. **Repent.**
   Turn away from every practice, object, or belief that
   dishonors God and opens a door to the enemy.
   Repentance isn't just saying, "I'm sorry." It's changing
   direction.

2. **Renounce.**
   Out loud, declare that you no longer belong to any false system or method of idolatry, whether it's astrology, Freemasonry, the Greek life, yoga, or something else. You are breaking the agreement with every practice you now understand is an offense to God.

3. **Remove.**
   Get rid of items tied to ungodly practices – charms, crystals, sage bundles, tarot cards, books, and any other items. Don't sell or donate them. Destroy them. Do as Josiah did in 2 Kings 23:24-25 and remove any item (or person) that is synonymous with witchcraft, and then turn to the Lord!

4. **Replace.**
   Fill your life and home with God's presence: worship, prayer, Scripture, and fellowship with other believers. Replace superstition with faith. Replace fear with truth. Replace old habits with holy and acceptable ones.

The prayer you will read in a moment is the most important prayer you will ever pray. It's not because the words are "eloquently written". It's because, if you say them with earnest intention and knowing that God hears you, you will walk away from this book having given your life to Jesus Christ.

As read in Chapter 3, Jesus said in John 14:6 (NIV):

> *"I am the way and the truth and the life. No one comes to the Father except through me."'*

> *"No one who denies the Son has the Father; whoever acknowledges the Son has the Father also." (1 John 2:23, NIV)*

That's a very bold and specific statement! The Bible clearly tells us that no other god can save except the Lord Jesus Christ! You may learn life lessons from the teachings of Buddha, Muhammad, Confucius, or whomever, but they won't get you into heaven.

"Jesus is 'the stone you builders rejected, which has become the cornerstone.' Salvation is found in no one else, for there is no other name under heaven given to mankind by which we must be saved." (Acts 4:11-22, NIV)

Simply being a "good person" is not enough. The Bible tells us in Isaiah 64:6 that our righteous acts are like filthy rags (think "menstrual cloths"). So, if we think we can be right with God because we're decent humans, we'll be in for a rude awakening when eternity hits. And eternity is a long time.

God doesn't want us to be guilty or condemned for eternity. That is why He sent His Son Jesus to die in our place for the sins WE have committed.

". . . for all have sinned and fall short of the glory of God." (Romans 3:23, NIV)

"For the wages of sin is death, but the gift of God is eternal life in Christ Jesus our Lord." (Romans 6:23, NIV)

"But God demonstrates his own love for us in this: While we were still sinners, Christ died for us." (Romans 5:8, NIV)

GOD HAS MADE A WAY! HALLELUJAH!

Before I give you the final prayer to pray from this book, let me give you one more important Scripture:

"If you declare with your mouth, 'Jesus is Lord,' and believe in your heart that God raised him from the dead, you will be saved. For it is with your heart that you believe and are justified, and it is with your mouth that you profess your faith and are saved. As Scripture says, 'Anyone who believes in him will never be put to shame. Everyone who calls on the name of the Lord will be saved.'" (Romans 10:9-11, 13 NIV)

Are you ready to pray out loud? If so, here we go!

Prayer: "Lord, your Word says that everyone has sinned, and that includes me. I can't get right with you by good works or human efforts, but you have made a way for me to have a relationship with you. You sent your Son Jesus to die for me – actually in my place for the things I did wrong. So, I confess that I have been a sinner. I confess that I need a Savior, and that Savior is Jesus Christ! I believe what your Word says – that Jesus died on the cross according to the Father's will. Jesus was buried, but He rose up again on the third day. Jesus is alive, and now so am I! Jesus, I give you my life and confess that you are Lord. Make what you want out of me. Cleanse me and use my life for your glory. I am yours now, God. I've prayed this in Jesus' name, amen."

👏 HALLELUJAH! 👏

If you prayed that prayer of surrender, I believe you are my brother or sister in Christ! Even if we never meet in person, we are part of the same body of Christ now. We will either meet one day on this earth or sometime in heaven! That is a comforting thought.

Although it is not specifically a Christian song, a lyric from the group McFadden & Whitehead comes to mind because it's so appropriate:

"Ain't no stopping us now, we're on the move!"

You belong to God now, and Jesus is going to do something wonderful in your life. How will living life for Jesus Christ look for you? Only time will tell the great things God will do for you and through you.

Promise Scriptures: *"Now to him who is able to do immeasurably more than all we ask or imagine, according to his power that is at work within us, to him be glory in the church and in Christ Jesus throughout all generations, for ever and ever! Amen." (Ephesians 3:20-21, NIV)*

"Who shall separate us from the love of Christ? Shall trouble or hardship or persecution or famine or nakedness or danger or sword? As it is written: "For your sake we face death all day long; we are considered as sheep to be slaughtered." No, in all these things we are more than conquerors through him who loved us. For I am convinced that neither death nor life, neither angels nor demons, neither the present nor the future, nor any powers, neither height nor depth, nor anything else in all creation, will be able to separate us from the love of God that is in Christ Jesus our Lord." (Romans 8:35-39)

"This day I call the heavens and the earth as witnesses against you that I have set before you life and death, blessings and curses. Now choose life, so that you and your children may live and that you may love the Lord your God, listen to his voice, and hold fast to him. For the Lord is your life, and he will give you many years in the land he swore to give to your fathers, Abraham, Isaac and Jacob." (Deuteronomy 30:19-20, NIV)

God loves you, and so do I.

About the Author

Sabrina Hamm is a business owner, author, and woman of faith with more than 20 years of entrepreneurial experience. In October 2005, she founded a company that grew over time and now serves numerous clients by God's grace. Sabrina's journey in business is proof that faith and diligence can build lasting success.

Sabrina's spiritual journey began long before her professional one. While she grew up with a knowledge of Jesus Christ and attended church with her mother and grandmother, God radically captured Sabrina's attention and led her to the confession of her sins, faith in Christ, and water baptism in the summer of 1999 – a life-changing sequence of events that continues to shape her life and mission today. Since then, Sabrina has served in various ministry capacities, and dedicates herself to serving in the marketplace; encouraging others through prayer and counsel; and helping people take God at His Word!

When she's not writing or overseeing her business, Sabrina enjoys life with her husband and children. You can also find Sabrina enjoying football (in front of the TV or at the stadium), cooking meals for anyone who will eat them, and singing or dancing for any reason at all. She wants everyone (that includes YOU) to remember that Jesus came not just to give us life, but life more abundantly!

(For more books, courses, and offerings from Sabrina, visit www.UntangleYourOptions.com.)

www.ingramcontent.com/pod-product-compliance
Lightning Source LLC
Chambersburg PA
CBHW070539130626
46555CB00003B/1496